LEGO CITY

Firefighters
to the Rescue

Welcome, LEGO fans!

LEGO® minifigures show you the world in a unique nonfiction program.

This book is part of a program of LEGO® nonfiction books, with something for all the family, at every age and stage. LEGO nonfiction books have amazing facts, beautiful real-world photos, and minifigures everywhere, leading the fun and discovery.

To find out more about the books in the program, visit www.scholastic.com.

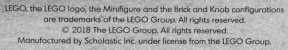

All rights reserved. Published by Scholastic Inc.,
Publishers since 1920. SCHOLASTIC and associated logos are
trademarks and/or registered trademarks of Scholastic Inc.

ISBN 978-1-338-28344-0

10 9 8 7 6 5 4 3 2 1   18 19 20 21 22

Printed in the U.S.A.   40
First edition, September 2018

The fire alarm sounds! Firefighters and their trucks are always ready for action. It's go time!

It can take two minutes to suit up. Some suits weigh 45 pounds (20 kg)—as much as a five-year-old child!

Fire suit, boots, helmet, and gloves.

A fire can be super-dangerous. We have special breathing gear and flame-proof suits.

It's a good thing I trained in the dark.

Build it!

Build a fire station. Fill it with firefighters and a fire truck ready to go.

Fire trucks are heavy. They can weigh as much as three elephants when loaded with crew and equipment.

A siren and flashing lights tell cars to get out of the way. A fire truck can travel at 75 miles per hour (120 km/h).

space for six firefighters

ladder

water tank

FIRE RESCUE

Emergency! To the fire truck! Sliding down a pole is way more fun than taking the stairs.

Someone needs rescuing. Make way, heroes coming through!

It might just be a garbage-can fire, but I need to put it out. Oops . . .

A fire truck holds enough water to put out a small fire. In a really big fire, the hose is connected to underground pipes.

Some hoses can stretch to 1,000 feet (300 m). Different hose nozzles can make hard jets, soft spray, or fine mist.

Build it!
Build a fire truck. What equipment does it carry?

Firefighters may have to suck the water out of people's swimming pools!

Sometimes, firefighters
must rescue people
or animals from
tall buildings.

They often use a cherry picker. This can stretch up to 100 feet (30 m)! The firefighter stands on a platform at the end of the ladder.

Smart puppy! Your warning bark told your family there was a fire.

That's what I call a helpful hound!

A forest fire can spread as fast as 14 miles per hour (22 km/h). The firefighters must put it out, fast.

Ground crew, the fire is heading northwest.

Eye in the sky, do you have a visual on the forest fire?

A helicopter drops firefighters near the fire. They clear the ground so the fire has nothing to burn.

Build it!

Build a fire helicopter. Make sure it's ready for takeoff!

Some helicopters can carry 2,800 gallons (10,600 liters) of water.

They hover over the fire and dump all the water in just four seconds.

Argghh! No more sizzling hotdogs, but at least the fire is out!

Build it!

Build a bright yellow fire plane, which can be seen whatever the weather.

In a huge fire, call the fire plane! It scoops up water from the ocean or a lake, without stopping. It takes 12 seconds to refill the tank.

The plane drops
the water on the
fire. Job done!
The fire is out.

The plane holds
500 bucketfuls
of water. It's known as
a super-scooper!

Fire boats are used to tackle fires on the shore, in the docks, or on a ship at sea. They pump water up from under the hull of the boat.

Fire boat to the rescue! We are here to save you!

Here's a life belt. Grab it! I'll pull you on board.

Go away! I don't need rescuing. I'm training for a race!

Fire boats speed across the water to rescue people. In stormy weather it can be a bumpy ride.

Build it!
Build a fire boat. What equipment will it carry?

FIREBOAT

4

There's a fire on a ship. The crew have all been rescued. Now the fire boats must put out the fire!

They work in teams to tackle the blaze. Each one can spray water 400 feet (122 m) in the air. Some fire boats spray a special foam to help put the fire out.

Build it!
Build a giant fire boat that is ready for an ocean rescue.

Some fire boats can pump 38,000 gallons (146,000 liters) of water per minute.

Hey! Watch where you point that hose!

19

The next emergency could be in a few minutes or a few hours' time. Firefighters and their trucks must always be ready.

Some firefighters might be eating or sleeping when the alarm sounds. Ring! Ring! Let's go save the day, again!

Being a firefighter is a tough job, but we love it. Stay safe, people!

Ah, time for a nice cup of coffee after a busy day . . .

Emergency! A cat is stuck up a tree. Make that coffee to go!

It looks quiet at the fire station. Use your stickers to turn it into an action station!

Glossary

blaze
A large fire that burns strongly.

cherry picker
A crane with a platform at the end for raising or lowering people.

docks
A place where ships stop for loading or unloading of goods, or for repairs.

fire station
The building where fire trucks and firefighting equipment are kept. It is also where firefighters wait until they are called to the next emergency.

fire suit
The special clothes firefighters wear to protect them from the heat of a fire.

hose
A flexible pipe for moving or spraying water.

hull
The main body part of a ship. It is mostly underwater.

nozzle
The spout at the end of a pipe or hose that is used to direct and control the flow of water.

pump
A machine used to raise up or move liquids (or sometimes, gases).

scoop
To pick up and move something quickly.

siren
A super-loud warning sound.

Credits

The publishers would like to thank:
For the LEGO Group: Randi Kirsten Sørensen, Senior Editorial Coordinator; Paul Hansford, Creative Publishing Manager; Martin Leighton Lindhardt, Publishing Graphic Designer; and Heidi K. Jensen, Business Manager.
For their help in making this book:
Neal Cobourne, John Goldsmid, Shari Joffe, Rachel Phillipson, Ali Scrivens, and Bryn Walls.
Photos ©: cover: Stefano Politi Markovina/Alamy Images; 1: kali9/iStockphoto; 2-3 fire engine: ryasick/iStockphoto; 2-3 background: Gang Zhou/iStockphoto; 3 top right: digitalhallway/iStockphoto; 4 background: maunger/iStockphoto; 4 inset: geargodz/iStockphoto; 5: Flashon Studio/Shutterstock; 6: welcomia/Shutterstock; 7: Nerthuz/Shutterstock; 8-9: koka55/Shutterstock; 10 left: ollo/iStockphoto; 10-11 bottom: ewg3D/iStockphoto; 10-11 background: deepblue4you/iStockphoto; 12 top: brazzo/iStockphoto; 12 bottom: gece33/iStockphoto; 14 left: Prathaan/iStockphoto; 14-15 top: Matteo Chinellato/Shutterstock; 14-15 bottom: Wustrow-K/iStockphoto; 15 top: Matteo Chinellato/Shutterstock;
16: geargodz/iStockphoto; 17: GBlakeley/iStockphoto; 18-19 water cannon: Ryan McGinnis/Alamy Images; 18 background: Ted Foxx/Alamy Images; 18 center left ship: everlite/iStockphoto; 19 water jet: PJ66431470/iStockphoto; 20: kali9/iStockphoto; 21: geargodz/iStockphoto; 22 center: ryasick/iStockphoto; 22-23 pavement: Gang Zhou/iStockphoto; 23 top: digitalhallway/iStockphoto; 23 bottom left: PJ66431470/iStockphoto; 23 bottom right: TRITOOTH/Thinkstock.

All LEGO illustrations and stickers by Paul Lee.

Thanks to all those brave firefighters out there!